Zoom In on
Dogs

Boxers

Leo Statts

abdopublishing.com

Published by Abdo Zoom™, PO Box 398166, Minneapolis, Minnesota 55439. Copyright © 2017 by Abdo Consulting Group, Inc. International copyrights reserved in all countries. No part of this book may be reproduced in any form without written permission from the publisher. Abdo Zoom™ is a trademark and logo of Abdo Consulting Group, Inc.

Printed in the United States of America, North Mankato, Minnesota
062016
092016

Cover Photo: Shutterstock Images
Interior Photos: Dora Zett/Shutterstock Images, 1; Lyubov Timofeyeva/Shutterstock Images, 5; Katho Menden/Shutterstock Images, 6; Mark Coffey/iStockphoto, 7; Dmitry Kalinovsky/Shutterstock Images, 8; Shutterstock Images, 9, 10–11, 13; Rolf Klebsattel/Shutterstock Images, 12, 19; Rita Kochmarjova/Shutterstock Images, 15; Jana Behr/Shutterstock Images, 16–17; Red Line Editorial, 20 (left), 20 (right), 21 (left), 21 (right)

Editor: Brienna Rossiter
Series Designer: Madeline Berger
Art Direction: Dorothy Toth

Publisher's Cataloging-in-Publication Data
Names: Statts, Leo, author.
Title: Boxers / by Leo Statts.
Description: Minneapolis, MN : Abdo Zoom, [2017] | Series: Dogs | Includes
    bibliographical references and index.
Identifiers: LCCN 2016941130 | ISBN 9781680791716 (lib. bdg.) |
    ISBN 9781680793390 (ebook) | ISBN 9781680794281 (Read-to-me ebook)
Subjects: LCSH: Boxer (Dog breed)--Juvenile literature.
Classification: DDC 636.73--dc23
LC record available at http://lccn.loc.gov/2016941130

Table of Contents

Boxers

Boxers are brave dogs.
They are smart and strong.

Some people say they are
named for the way they play.
They stand on their back legs.

They use their front paws. It looks like they are boxing.

7

Boxers are muscular.

They have square heads.
Their ears can be pointed
or **floppy**.

A boxer's fur
is short.

It can be fawn and brindle. It can also be black or white. Brushing keeps it shiny.

Care

Boxers need lots of exercise. They should be taken on walks.

They need toys to play with.

Personality

Boxers are playful.
They have lots of energy.
They can jump very high.
Many like to play fetch.

Boxers are good watch dogs. They are alert and loyal. They protect their owners.

Boxers are a mix of bulldogs and **mastiffs**. They come from Germany.

They **herded** cattle. Later they were used in police work.

19

Average Weight

A male boxer is heavier than a full suitcase.

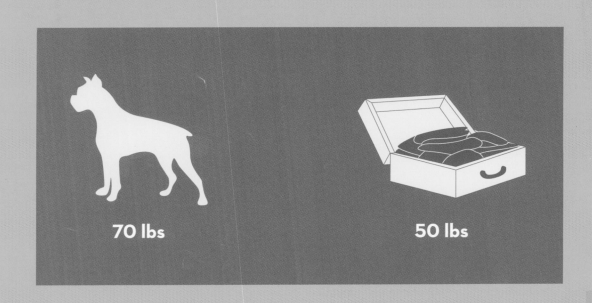

70 lbs

50 lbs

Average Height

A male boxer is shorter than an acoustic guitar.

2 ft

3 ft 4 in

Glossary

brindle - a gray, tan, or tawny color with darker streaks or spots.

fawn - a light yellowish-brown color.

floppy - limp and hanging loosely.

herded - moved animals together in a group.

loyal - faithful to a person or idea.

mastiff - a breed of big dogs with short, smooth fur.

Booklinks

For more information
on boxers, please visit
booklinks.abdopublishing.com

 In on Animals!

Learn even more with the Abdo Zoom
Animals database. Check out
abdozoom.com for more information.

Index